trying
×
trying

Also by Dora Malech

Poetry

Shore Ordered Ocean
Say So
Stet
Soundings: Selected Poems
Flourish
Trying × Trying

Translation

Dolore Minimo by Giovanna Cristina Vivinetto, translated with Gabriella Fee

Edited Collection

The American Sonnet: An Anthology of Poems and Essays, edited with Laura T. Smith

trying × trying

Dora Malech

Carnegie Mellon University Press
Pittsburgh 2025

ACKNOWLEDGMENTS

The author would like to thank the editors of the following publications in which these poems first appeared:

Birmingham Poetry Review: "From the Dance," "verum factum"
The Hopkins Review: "Diebenkorn, *Ocean Park*"
Ink Node: "The News"
Lana Turner: "Travelogue"
LARB Quarterly: "Ablation," "Gwass"
Memorious: "Abbr. Bestiary," "Elegy"
Modern Language Studies: "Aletheia," "Color Study," "Confessional," "In Western Massachusetts," "Living Situation," "*Perfect for those corrections in a hurry!*"
The Napkin Poetry Review: "whether"
On the Seawall: "Dispatch," "Monumental Life Building," "Reflexive," "saw, circular"
POETRY: "Niqqud"
Poetry International: "The Forecast," "Last Ultrasound," "Nesting," "New Recipe," "With the House to Myself"
Smartish Pace: "Early Evening," "Secret Song," "Timeline"
Two Peach: "Rearview Mère"

Some of the poems in this book—"Address, Delivered," "After 'After Us,'" "Animal Crossing," "Dream Recurring," "History," "How to Make It," "Iris Park," "Torah Study," "Tried,"—were first published in *Time Trying*, a folio commissioned for *Four Quartets: Poetry in the Pandemic* (Tupelo Press, 2020). Thanks to Jeffrey Levine and Kristina Marie Darling.

"All the Stops" was first published in *The Southampton Review* and reprinted in *The Best American Poetry* (Scribner, 2021). Thanks to Cornelius Eady, Emily Gilbert, David Lehman, and Tracy K. Smith.

"Standards-Based Assessment" was first published as part of the Poetry Foundation's *PoetryNow* radio series. Thanks to Michael Slosek.

The poems in this book inspired by Vicente Gerbasi—"Arrangement," "At Times," "*Y*," "*Cuando, cuando*"—were written at the invitation of and first published by *Atlantean Poets*. Thanks to Beverly Pérez Rego.

The International Writing Program at the University of Iowa commissioned "Travelogue" for its Book Wings performance initiative, later included in *Book Wings: A Virtual Drama* (Autumn Hill Books, 2015). Thanks to Christopher Merrill, Ash Davidson, and Nate Brown.

Book design by So Young Park

Library of Congress Control Number 2025931893
ISBN 978-0-88748-711-8

Printed and bound in the United States of America

10 9 8 7 6 5 4 3 2 1

for Ada + Morris

Contents

Dream Recurring

All eyes turn doorward
toward me.
                This is History.
Where are you supposed to be?

Attempted Haiku

The nation is holding its breath . . .
—*NYT*, January 17, 2021

Breath, yes, but what else
can we hold? Water, space for,
accountable, fire?

Reflexive

The teacher told me
my heart was roughly
the size of my fist

and I saw my hand
clench around
the new knowledge

as if with an infant
instinct again,
simian vestige,

palm and fingers
gripping phantom
fur midair

between two trees.
It's natural the visible
endure as measure

of the hidden,
but to this day
it sways in me

not only sense
of scale but purpose,
for what is the heart

if not called from
the start to close
over, to cling to,

to hang on, to hold
itself to this day,
this day, this day,

this day, this day,
this day, this day,
this day, this day

Standards-Based Assessment

I.

Nothing *happened* here.
Meaning it was *done.*

Over counts itself among
the studied synonyms

but beyond
those round mouths

opening for answers
done is the opposite of *over.*

II.

What is the sum
when you add

cut flowers in cellophane
to teddy bears and prayers

and the difference
when you take away

and take away
and take away?

Show your work.
Attend to precision.

III.

The students are gone.
It is not summer.

The classroom snake
that fled its shattered tank

the long shadows
draping themselves over

the overturned desks
and the red pen fallen

to the floor will count
as symbols on a different

subject test. Let them be
innocent in this world.

Confessional

It seems the first use of the term in our
aesthetic sense was in Rosenthal's review
of Lowell's *Life Studies*, in which he described
the book as "a series of personal
confidences, rather shameful, that one
is honor-bound not to reveal." That was
in 1959, my mother was
eight years old, and for her, the word was still
physical, a place into which she didn't
want to go. If her story holds, it seems
that she was born pre-lapsed (quite the opposite
of prelapsarian), a knock-kneed natural
heretic, pint-size apostate disguised
in pleated plaid. The nuns instructed her
to pray for the martyred saints, and she prayed
to never be a martyred saint, which I
take as an early sign of her capacity
for pleasure, a nature she nurtured through
adult authority's cruelty and neglect,
carried across the ocean into her own
grown self to pass that nature and that nurture
on to me. A poem's the only shadowed
box I've ever entered to tell my truths
to a stranger. I tell my mother plenty,
but not everything. The same goes for what
I'll tell the poem. Some secrets are *rendered*
speechless. "Don't minimize your evil," she says
the priest would say to her through the dark screen.

verum factum

a flaw I follow seems
seam's source sutured

soldered line of scar-shine's
old itch good as knew

Unaccompanied Minor

My feet can reach
the pedals now,

but still I go
nowhere.

Right foot
down is just

a longer sound,
one chord held to

its unsung song
about the road.

Living Situation

My roommate would return home late
from Bible study group at Denny's,
smelling of syrup, saying prayer's

what matters most right now. The first
time I tried ecstasy it didn't
kick in until hours after

I'd swallowed the pill, danced sober
with strangers, and, disappointed,
returned at dawn, only to double

over and vomit on the steps
at the entryway. I wiped my mouth
and went upstairs and crawled

beneath the sheet with pupils dilated
despite the sunrise, rubbing the rough,
miraculous nubs of the stucco wall

with my fingertips and turning to gaze
at Tina sleeping, washed in goodwill
toward her and imagining what her faith

might feel like, like a flickering pilot
light inside her body, or like
the low-tide certain lap of wavelets

in a day-warmed bay. All that
early morning, I thought I knew
it must have some relationship

with heat or light. Later, a huge
fish swam to the surface
of the rag rug between our beds,

terrifying and benevolent. The whole
next week, whenever my face could find
a moment alone, it started crying.

Color Study

See (hear) how the objects of the world
echo as tone from stone, as tint from woad
or weld or madder, one primary palette
placed, while elsewhere the sum of silks
and sea snails' brilliant bruising deepens
beneath the sun.

                                        Or we might liken this
listening to lichen's litmus, vivid test,
intoxicating paradox that blinds
us in a sense, orchil's liquor brewed
not to stain lip drowsy but to shade
eye bloodshot from the outside in, thrown dye
still splashing back history's fluid hue
or fluid terms at least, a spectrum spilling
deep red into blue.

                                              Keep in mind
that lichens aren't plants, but partnerships.
To the composite, add urine, potash, lime,
and gypsum. Steep leaves and cool the liquid
quickly and then strain. Spines spiral to
spire on a predator capable
of purple.

                        Later, on this loom, warp makes
waves, sound realized in ictus, slashed
to its sense as it's sentenced to time: line.
Syllable's roots now grounded in a taking
together of letters, massed beneath a struck
branch splintering into fire, not refuge from
a rain of breves, rather enter that blow
that shocks the scene to light

(and dark—
cultures' colors' firsts, so often followed
by a flash and gash of red. An opening,
or a punishment for insisting on binaries
and dividing from the first? In language,
it seems blue came later. Did we still know
it in us, wordless, all along? Throb in
a vein, as when Camus writes: *When I look*
at my life and its secret colors, I feel like
bursting into tears. Like that sky.
It's rain and sun both, noon and midnight.)

In saying, saying skews to light makes (slants
to) sight, though even without, following
the vats' decomposing stench along
the shoreline, we might feel forward
into last sense's license took to tongues,
a taste choired back somatic to re-scent
and retouch, revisions that resound.

Diebenkorn, *Ocean Park*

Baltimore Museum of Art

Here, the charge between the colors hums,
homing, where two blues fuse and square themselves.
Outside inside, vertical lines throb *come*
while horizontals steady, sturdy shelves,
and each diagonal exhales potential,
Adam's finger reaching out at what might
not, here, need to be any God at all,
but rather, glorious lowercase light.
Lavender isosceles points upward
from the lower left-hand corner toward
cadmium, cobalt. Charcoal girders grid
architectonic streak and stroke. Unpeopled
here, one may, alone but not lonely,
meet and hold the eye inside geometry.

In Western Massachusetts

The sky and snowfall blaze the same.
Lack of contrast tips the ground up
into two dimensions, blank greeting
card folded open at the horizon's crease
and tacked to whatever wall's behind it all.

The glare insinuates itself inside the skull,
flares to my stare. Or gaze? The seeming
synonyms separate sight to spectrum,
reverberate and mark vision's division
obscene or simply scene, a picture or

a monster. Picture Dickinson's papers'
proximity, fascicles' little decussations
marking lexical variants like linguistic
arithmetic, or buried treasure, or
children's graves in winter. Go ahead

and call her papers "alabaster." Recall
the appalling pallor of Melville's whale.
Appraise Du Bois's "wages of whiteness"
still paid out every day, into my pocket too,
seemingly as natural as weather,

seemingly as slippery to refuse.
I could drive an hour or so and pay
to enter her Homestead bedroom,
try on her "miles of Stare" or
"Heaven in a Gaze." In the restoration,

they found no poems beneath her
floorboards, just a needle and a pin.
"The maddest dream—recedes—

unrealized." Or else "the nearest dream—
recedes—unrealized." Or ten minutes

to Melville's Arrowhead to see
the small room that bore the oceans
and Leviathans. Or twenty to Du Bois's
boyhood home, which isn't there.
Pines, a parking area, a path, a kiosk,

a plaque, remains of a foundation.
The scholar writes, "In essence,
by the early 1960s Du Bois's and his
family's presence had been erased
from the New England landscape."

A 1969 homesite dedication drew
"at least thirty threats to blow up
or destroy the memorial."
Closed eyes, but the blaze stays.
Wherever I look is looking away.

The News

Now's news begins with babies on the way. Just one's inside me, but another's ascending to the throne our nation prides itself on not having, though among our American ways and means is "if you build it" etcetera, and this one claims he knows from building. The New Year's too a baby of a kind, since ancient Greece at least, then Jesus-ized in Germany, secularized to any-baby and captured as such by the *Saturday Evening Post* and past decades of animated cels, so the sashed, top-hatted, and diaper-clad remains today what last year Lisa Rose of CNN called "an avatar of optimism . . . [h]is enduring appeal . . . the embodiment of hope that the next twelve months will be better than the last." Now that I'm growing one from scratch, I fear I feel the metaphor extend, the headlines bearing now-familiar nausea, cramps, fatigue, and shooting pains at sudden movements, as if the coming years aren't stork-dropped bundles but bloody bulks that won't pass through without a fight. A gray day, and I can see my lamp-lit face reflected in the window at noon. The top stories swim through me and I dive deep to breathe below the fold, ashamed at my gratitude for the teeming triviality: "The Story of Weihnachtsgurke" . . . "Thieves with Discriminating Taste Steal Sable Furs From New York Shop." For a moment, all the babies sleep, and I forget responsibility inside and out of me. It's Christmas morning again, and my only urgency is searching for that porcelain half-sour hidden in the evergreen, and then . . . and then . . . and then . . . I'm running past the broken glass, cheek pressed to the haul of pelts, arms weighted with the precious dead.

Nesting

Nest*ing*—with emphasis on process,
a final phoneme humming at its work.
It's in the endless present of it. Some days,
I feel like I've never encountered a noun,
proper or otherwise. To try to build a resting
place is restless business, unfinished, always
an errant twig, an open mouth, and then
the stiff wind of a changing season. This is
the present, as in the clichéd gift that keeps
on giving, though giving mostly sounds too gentle
for these moments thrown: think fast. It's playing
catch with both hands bound behind your back.
It's yours only as it whizzes through you instantly
re-gifted as purview and province of the past.

Last night, homes were yanked away midair,
or at borders ordered inside airports before
or after flights, a soaring feeling falling,
crashed. The father saying to his crying
daughters, sit down. Drink some water. In a
pocket, an amulet meant for a future in Baltimore
or Nashville, a hand held tight, sweat on metal.
Hand of Fatima, Miriam, Mary, apotropaic—
though here the apotropaism's been perverted,
not malicious spirits or the evil
eye warded off, but fathers, mothers,
neighbors, children, babies turned away
from our country like so much bad luck. What we
infer in fear. An averted eye, indeed.

Alternate Genesis: No green branch. No land.
And the dove hovering over the waters indefinitely,
or returning to the ark to die at sea.

Perfect for those corrections in a hurry!

Meet these eyes, *I*s, and ayes,

who sees, is, and sanctions,

those that, as we say, *have it*

(out and/or in for), justice's

blindfolded figurine refigured

for what Wite-Out® renders illegible,

advertises as *no fuss, no mess.*

Stroke on easily and evenly to cover,

though sometimes it takes

a double-coat double-down,

raised from the page like scar tissue.

Utopic myopia, myopic utopia,

luxury of seeing the gate half open,

hinge rusted at a preposition's

assumption *(for your protection).*

We are our own worst

witness, witless, as if

checking the closet for ghosts—

see, honey, I don't see anything.

Apostrophe as possession, omission,

address (with roots in a turning

away): can t. As in, what we don't
know   hurt us. As in, *I   breathe.*

Address, Delivered

Term of crumpled paper scrawled with false starts out this essay we will in this essay we will this term to mean more than the sum of its partitions no say can I say ramifications' roots and branches as in plant a flag and sow the soil ours poll pole as no fixed point to guide us but a trunk running rings or stuffed with plunder plant a flag and it grows each limb as consequence to ramify again in purple foothills swapped at birth for a cross and tendered to the touch to ratify a term that never looked inside to see that it was made of its own ending now how can we claim we didn't feel its onus in us this missed miscarriage of that which we willed our ears to mishear swore our oath on a book of holes wore that dress we claimed in white and gold when all along the truth was black and blue as any other region of injury just a striped piece of cloth aloft but enough to show our shape proudly hate to make this figure belong to any body but it's what's still on hand and what we have our hands on still inside us stilled inside us *pure products* of now and how can we say that this was never ours or anything that we once wanted when we have carried it in us for so long

History

I felt I carried something in me
and cared for it accordingly

with vitamins and pride. I won't
say what I named it, but I named it

out loud. Then, no heartbeat.
Whatever it was wasn't and never

was. Don't look at me with pity.
You know you've known

its name and how it feels to hold
inside you and believe it to be

good, and growing, only to learn
that it was nothing all along.

Nothing, but much bloodier.

Arrangement

after Vicente Gerbasi, "El leopardo"

The hunters take the leopard's skin
and spread it to the wind, a constellation.
When the night leads them deeper into
its fugue of leaves and vines they follow
like lovers who can't bring themselves
to ask who else it has been holding close.
Its hands are so warm,
so warm, and the fireflies flare
like the blown embers of memory,
courage held captive
until only its rage remains.

Aletheia

A long-gone hand behind this scrap of map
dips the brush into red lead again
and lifts the wet tip up to fly across
an ocean and touch down in the unknown
where it emblazons its best guesses, draws
ornate conclusions in the far shore's sand.

Now, as ever, dawn illuminates
the landscape's manuscript, over which
the day must pass, peripatetic, before
sunset can rubricate the hour's red letter.

There are still shapes and patterns we are taught
truth takes, contested borders unexpressed,
pretty pictures in complimentary
colors, nations nestled purple against
yellow, crimson cradling blue. What hand
wants to smudge the fine lines and express
the messiness of lives lived liminal?

The globe at least attempts to hold a kind
of truth, dimensionality, orb
born of glued gores narrowing their finer
points poleward, but when the spinning stops,
it's still a toy that tumbles into the same
traps of empire and HIC SVNT LEONES.

I'm not immune to putting the crypt- before
the cart- in all my -ography. In my
heart of hearts, I call my aorta
regina viarum, the Appian Way,
beg each ornery orrery to orbit
me.

Rubbing my closed eyes in the dark,
I might think that I see lights, when in fact
I feel pressure and cells activate
phosphene's entoptic phenomenon, bright
blurs like what a satellite might capture,
whole galaxies or our metropolises'
light pollution, depending where the camera
sets its sights.

Deep beneath the ocean's
swells, bioluminescent creatures
travel currents as predators and prey,
and a black box flight recorder pings its signal
outside the range of human hearing.

I've heard
the box is actually painted orange.

I've heard we have thirty days before
the batteries die and it falls silent.

If we were to trust our actual ears,
we'd think it had been silent all along.

Abbr. Bestiary

Ripped page
docks tail, crops
ear into a new
morality, wild

and bewildering
as the first,
lacuna's lecture

in extremities'
extremis, object's

altered lesson,

as if less were
best in show,

leaves brittled
and unbound,
ex-codex wrecked

irreversibly, thus
resurrected into
parchment's
favorite parable.

Adam rendered
hemless hovers
above former feet,
element-defeated,

amputated into
the blank space past
where the image

ends, in which
the now-invisible

animals lay waiting

for the curse or
blessing of a name.

New math
says this torn
pard—real leopard's

imaginary half—
is now a quarter
creature and freer
for it, says lines

of horse permute
to lines of shore,
a jagged absence.
To those who'd

want to hide in
hide or hold tail's
tale, I say let go

and look below.
A see-through

sea's bright side

laps at a world of
virtues and of vices

unmoored bodiless,
no herd or flock to
cower or to crow,

murder excised
and pride elided.
That roar you hear
is just eternity.

Niqqud

A real reader would find
the vowels expendable,
mere diacritic spoor
on a path worn right
to left by sacred sense,

but I still cling to handle
and doorknob, lurch
stone to stone without
seeing the stream, pick
at each spot until it scars—

paw print, dead-end road,
bullet hole, ball falling
down the stairs, distant
planet, dropped crutch—
I can't even remember

their names, except shva,
which sticks somehow:
a dot on a dot like a colon
preceding explanation,
though it falls un-followed

here, un-sound or nearly,
deferral, demurral, rest or
restlessness, catch in
the throat at a question
I can't begin to ask.

Y

after Vicente Gerbasi, "Canto I"

Venimos de la noche y hacia la noche vamos.
Our journey hangs on a letter's hinge.
It sentences its sentence to itself, a life
in prism through which all our minor
refractions flash back and back.
Its form bears, but barely, the weight
of the losses slung across its shoulders.
Its point drills a hole in stone like the one
we saw at the foot of the frame
in the old country's ruins where once
a revolving door turned at a touch.
Atrás queda . . . Atrás quedan . . . Atrás quedan . . .
Atrás quedan . . . Atrás quedan . . . Atrás queda . . .
Our list of what is gone goes on, extinguishes
itself in the effort of trying to distinguish night
from night, wrest rest from its forever home.
The letter aims like a slingshot, fires not simply
stones but almond tree, leopard, lakes, graves
at the foot of the cypresses' hexed forests
throwing their own blue shadows back.
In the valleys, the flowers wake in tears
but can't describe this dream that they keep
having. *Pero*—the rope that binds, perfects
its one tight task, all the while wishing
itself a wick. The letter flicks
its forked tongue. As it advances,
it holds its arms up high, gesturing
through emptiness as if across
a crowded room. It is a wishbone
wondering which way to break.
Silt stirs at the confluence of its rivers.

Elegy

I want to start *the story*
goes, but then the story
stops. I want to say you

borrowed Chekhov's gun,
but it was just American,
a dumb Colt bucking in

your hand, neither of you
old enough to know
better, both ready to run.

Speed is ignorant of direction,
says the physics text.
The part I love about

the story that I hate is
when it seems you still
believe in what comes

next, just not for you,
is when, after you
drink a beer and before

you, as they say, *do*
yourself in, meaning out
of this world worth

saving, you pause
to place the can
in the recycling bin.

From the Dance

Remember the boy
who swallowed the pin

from someone's corsage
and came back to the prom

later that night with the X-ray
to prove it? His name faded out

like the end of a radio hit,
but his hospital wristband's

dazzling grin in the blacklight
remains. Whatever song I play,

he keeps writhing, shirt
sweat-wet and face shining

like something sharp is still
inside him inside me—

All the Stops

Rolling through the intersection, I see in my rearview
the back of the familiar octagon rusted over, belying
the option of following its forward-facing order.

The driver behind me brakes just as half-heartedly,
and for a moment I pretend together we'd make one
whole heart's best effort to postpone the hurt and hurtle

past the red fur of thorn and bud beyond the shoulders
as the season nips the next one's heels. IF YOU CAN'T
SEE MY MIRRORS I CAN'T SEE YOU warns the sticker

affixed to the glint of the bumper ahead, but I've only got
eyes for the peripheral blood smear shimmer where
whatever winter took is finally kicking in. All those years

wishing I were sure and thin as a sign and could wait
for no mandible nor manager nor manna nor mention.
All those years I told my charges to hold my hand

and look both ways as I told myself to stop at nothing.
Don't let go. Let go. Everywhere, the referents of other
people's safe words—dive bars dropping paint flakes

and first flowers face down with the sun on their napes.
A tinge of desperation in every command. Take it
from me. Ahead a sky scored by some flight's velocity,

contrail kindred in its substance—water, pressure. Two lights
at a complicated crossing and the capitals cry THIS IS YOUR

SIGNAL. Sure, but there are other shapes in me, flipped
evergreen like rare old color film and just as quick to burn.

saw, circular

we serve

the swerve that one
good turn

deserves. another

riven swivel,
pivot fodder.

the whole flock

reverses charges,
calls collective.

turn me

on to turn me
one again.

how in

our moment's *um*,
now buckles,

bones up on

the autopsy-turvy
table, espies

and pries the gum

stuck under
to make a meal

of then recoil,

anguine, sanguine,
disavow each

season's treason

as it reveals
the wheel.

New Recipe

If you're really
asking what I want

for dinner, dear,
a carrot or a stick

of butter doesn't
matter to this batter

none. The dough's
in what you do,

not herb but verb.
Imperatives' essentials

oil the pan, and so,
forgo the grocery list

and stay, puree, a while.
The only ingredients

that can't be swapped
for applesauce or air

are the stir inherent
in your wrist, and

of course, to taste,
your tongue.

whether

a future read aloud
spells out a could

without you
in your element
leaves cold
as our or

and even
with remains
a wintery mix as

sleet stung one
unsettles gone

potential ever forecast
in a chance of cloud

Tried

on the floor before
a party at which
no one thought

much about shared air
the virus still elsewhere
or we thought the virus

still a far fear
and my body
telling me it

was time to try
I won't go into
detail a certain

detail was my body
telling me to try and
the calendar agreed

we call it a window
let's try in the window
as if it's public work

spectacle like we have
a show to show for our
effort or wares to display

funny to think of February's
as the year's last parties
leap we say as if we're

trying to urge it all over all
evening I drank fizzy water
and tried to believe in cells

like those bubbles
something going
are you trying are

you trying are you
trying bright inside
of me and beyond

lay the lie lodged deep
in believe and the sting
of a thing that could be

At Times

after Vicente Gerbasi, "Canto V"

My ear pressed to the wall,
I can't tell if you recall or recoil.
Listening long after you fall
silent, my thoughts draw
the sadness you described
as an animal I've seen
only in pictures. It crouches
cornered, plays dead until
it believes itself to be a clock
of stone or a flag in a language
with no need for a word for wind,
though I heard you say
how it runs when you lunge.

Timeline

I.

You started with nothing but intention,
then the ghost of a pink line creeping
behind the first in the wand's window
like my morning eyes conjured double,
then twinge and ache. Sweet someone
waiting in, I, on, secret willed to keep.

II.

Returning later to the clot of lines above
like a lump in the notebook's throat
I know there is no you. Nor was. Another
wand in me can stir no life. Sterile gavel.
This is medicine, not magic. I was grown
home with no owner, a warm waterbed
and blood bath drawn, an empty carriage
pulled along by hope over the stones.

Cuando, cuando

after Vicente Gerbasi, "Canto XII"

Father of my loneliness and of my poetry,
time is an open question here. Your life
and your death lodge together, split
the rented room of my heart.
Some nights they stay out
until dawn and I let myself believe
them gone, imagining I might
sleep in, dreamless, then spend
the day sweeping the place clean,
painting over the marks on the walls.
Then the light lowers its fists to play
all its notes at once and I know
they have returned, bearing
that old summons
in a dense agitation of dark blue horses.

Iris Park

How many times have I typed
"dead" for "dear" this spring?
Enough. My loss, less art than
craft this spring, a name spelled

out in uncooked noodles and glue
pitched in the kitchen trash,
construction paper steeped in dregs,
bent corner dabbing at potatoes' eyes,

ripped edge wicking the last juice
from a brown core. Outside,
rain is pestering the little
leaves again and flooding

the road my mind drives back
north to the hospital, where each
precast concrete parking structure
is named after a flower.

How to Make It

All my friends are now at a distance,
overwhelmed with work and world and care,

injustice, filled with fear of bills and illness,
running scared though going nowhere and so,

of course, taking on more chores by other
names: some contorting toward the E chord on

their new mail-order ukulele fretboards,
others wielding hooks and needles to pull

hats and scarves from skeins of yarn through spring
and into summer, or coddling green fleets

of cotyledons to life in hope of herbs
and flowers, yes, but also just to tend

some simpler lives writ bright in potting soil,
and one with palms planted easing her knees

up her shaking arm toward side crow pose,
another shaking shots and ice and adding

-tini or -rita to each concoction's end,
and another beating cream of tartar

into egg whites aspiring to alpine
range as part one of step two of nine

in a thirteen-ingredient recipe
to bake the perfect homemade yodel cake, while

elsewhere behind my own closed door I restart
the video of Yodel 101

with yodeler Wylie Gustafson who makes
a song out of the place we break over and

over again. What luck each time he asks
me *to warm up with a dejected sigh.*

With the House to Myself

Today, I am the bubble in a level
set atop a picture hung askew,
someone's eye on a cornflower sky

and a field of stover still to be silaged,
a scene reaped not as agriculture and
forecast not as weather, rather saved

simply in an archive of yellow and blue.
These specimens unlabeled mad, sad,
happy, holy here just are. As much as

possible, no meanings accrue. Is this
why the shot can't rise to art, or might
I not be troubling myself sufficiently?

Remember, in this scenario I'm just
the level's bubble. Without your hands,
even the horizon is an uphill battle.

This is one of a few things I would like
to straighten out before company comes.

Secret Song

The buttercups'
and dandelions'
yellow lights blink
on with the season.

Little hypocrites,
my hearts, who
want a wild life
the color of caution.

Torah Study

At more than one synagogue, congregants received an email this week asking them to no longer kiss the Torah scroll in reverence.
—*NYT*, March 9, 2020

Sweet skeptic, nonbeliever
for whom I never

wrote a vow, not wanting
to fuss and press at the us of us,

not wanting to conscript and constrict
into some narrow stripe of service,

years into this, I've found
the words and want

to recommit as such. I don't believe
that it's too much to ask. Here goes.

My atheist, may I die,
some distant day, your holy

book, your sacred text: ancient,
full of poetry, and often kissed.

Dispatch

The end of day
bays in the blood.

It has caught
a great lack

and will not rest
until I close

the distance.

Animal Crossing

I.

> *In my dreams*
> *the snouts drool on the marble,*
> *suffering children, suffering flies,*
> *suffering the consumers*
> *who won't meet their steady eyes*
> *for fear they could see.*
>
> —Philip Levine, "Animals Are Passing from Our Lives"

I've never played it, but I've seen
the game's name everywhere this spring,
though by everywhere I really
mean the screens where I sought solace
when the pandemic pushed us all
inside. The name repeats inside
my brain, rifling through for loose
referents, fair game, and finds

Midwestern penguins wandering
not free but freer through the empty
halls of closed aquariums
and museum galleries, taking
in the glint off schools of fish
and Venetian altarpieces,

the hopeful hoax dolphins supposedly
swimming the canals of Venice,
or rather, the real dolphins
filmed in the Mediterranean
hundreds of miles from the bronze lion
spreading his centuries-old wings
over Piazza San Marco,

the Bronx Zoo's flesh-and-blood lions
and tigers symptomatic, coughing
dry coughs, refusing to eat, testing
positive for the not-animal
of the virus replicating
its seemingly insatiable
not-appetite to not-live on,

the red knot sandpipers headed
toward the Arctic hungry this May,
their usual horseshoe crab egg feast
on the shores of the Delaware Bay
foiled by this year's colder water
and storm-slowed spawning,

and the rows of horseshoe crabs
just inland inside the Lonza biotech
facility, steel needles draining
bottles of their milky blue blood
for its primeval sensitivities,
as any vaccine made for us will
need to pass their ancient assay first.

II.

> *A grey light coming on at dawn,*
> *No fresh start and no bird song*
> *And no sea and no shore*
> *That someone hasn't seen before.*
> —Philip Levine, "A New Day"

Finally venturing out again in June,
I sing my way across the Bay Bridge,
radio up and windows down.
I get some distance, keep my distance.

Shells and telsons litter the littoral
zone, a little literal litter
too, a plastic bag that echoes
THANK YOU, which I pincer
gingerly between my thumb
and forefinger to trek back up
across the hot sand and toss
in the bins by the dunes. The rest
I see, I leave. I'm sweaty from
my one good deed. Pelicans skim
in formation. One tern returns another's
reprimand. Later I hang my
clothes on the line, but nothing dries
completely this close to the sea.

III.

> *Somewhere beyond the Flood*
> *We wandered hand in hand*
> *In a country we remember*
> *Somewhere in our blood . . .*
> —Philip Levine, "Who Are You?"

I confess that this is not a game
and should be over, but I don't
know how long it takes to play
what's not a game. I admit I asked
the neighbor's clumsy cat if any
body can live on feathers alone
as she crouched against
my steps again below the
round mouths of the perfect
holes the carpenter bees keep

boring because even my wooden
railing remains unfinished.

The kaddish never mentions death,
but we know when we need to say it,
the viddui too, confession,
though there's no confession in
the Hebrew Bible as a noun,
not something but something to do,
for example, to lay hands
upon the head of a living goat
and confess a nation's sins upon it.

The copyrighted syllables
run on, chyronic elegy
on the head-in-handheld
disconsolate console of my mind,
shibboleth-for-one each time
that rhythm is or isn't in
my sights, its stresses landing heavy
on its "a" and "cross" with the rest
of each word padding obediently
behind. The belts and hooks begin
again to bear the bodies and
the parts of bodies past the workers
standing shoulder to shoulder for
our appetites, the virus lingering
in the frigid indoor air,
the virus hitching a ride home
on company buses, belying the execs'
beliefs in their versions of processing
and of power, in plastic and in palatable
names—those first tests on animals
performed in Eden's biotech facility—

those sounds we made with our own
mouths to put things in their place,
those mouths of ours that now—still
now—are even deadly when we sing.

The Forecast

I turn back from the page to the window,
beyond which it has started to snow, something

almost sweet—confectionary. My unborn
baby basks in her microclimate, oblivious

to other weather, other worlds. I can feel
the little taps as if she's swimming laps,

pushing off from either end of the heated
pool. All day yesterday, I tried to tune

out the endless steno of the gutters'
melting, but the dive in temperature

has silenced that, frozen the world to a held
breath so the space inside of me, the house,

sounds loud again, and I can't tell the background
roar of my own body from the electric

hum of the appliances. The snow that first
appeared as powdered sugar now seems

a single-ply sheet of gauze—the first, a view
that can console but not nourish, the second,

capable of stanching a flow if folded over
and over on itself—but this one scrim alone

as draped across the scene outside would bloom
with blood, a wet net holding nothing in

an instant. I see I've turned a winter idyll to an
open mouth and open wound again. All day

yesterday, I tried to tune out the news, or rather
to consume without being consumed, to float

in the stream and absorb what I needed,
resist being pulled under and then even

farther down. Where was Heraclitus
when I needed him? Asleep in a book

I couldn't find, asleep on a somewhere shelf
with stars on his margins, as bold children

used to draw on the faces of their friends
fallen first asleep. The flakes accumulate,

disappear the once-crisp horizontals
of a bench into the ground beyond,

simplifying edge and depth to a scrap
of a blank page, a note passed unwritten.

Last Ultrasound

The wand warms to me while your pieces swim
into focus. Where I would want to find, first,
your face, the technician is after numbers now

instead, zeroing in on measurements, dragging
circles across her screen to circumscribe your head
and abdomen, taking her virtual ruler to your femur.

I have to trust we'll have time soon enough
for your close-ups in person, for me to catalog
your features framed in air instead of water.

For now, there's your liver. There's the arch
of your beating heart. In the scan's earlier
iterations of past months and weeks, the tech

indulged us, lingered on your fingers and on
your profile's pose, zoomed in on the wavelet
of your nose and out to catch your body

in its entirety curled inward like a shrimp,
let us take, as souvenir, a glossy picture strip
not unlike the one that I insisted on taking

with your father—far before a moment when
I could have called him that, as I tentatively
practice doing now—when I fed my dollars

into the slot, pulled back the curtain and pulled
him into the photo booth at the boardwalk arcade.
Back out past the Skee-Ball, Whac-a-Mole,

and shooting games, I stood with my back to
the breeze from the ocean to protect the evidence,
pored over our particulars—this smile, that kiss—

caught in black and white. The transducer glides
across me one more time, catching your ribs,
which flash bright slats across the screen

like sunbeams filtering outward, playing
through the currents that cross the shards
and innards of a galleon submerged. In this figure,

I'll be the wreck so you can be the treasure.
Or—weighted, weightless, waiting—we can all
simply converge on the scene as fellow divers—

the you that's in me now, the you that I'll meet
later, the sonographer, your father, and I—each
navigating depths in search of some shine or shape

that we might have the strength or nerve to call
by name and thereby haul up to the surface
and claim as such as known, our own.

Ablation

Those months when I was making
milk

I tried
each time
to find

a figure to make sense of the sensation.
The baby's warm, steady mouth needed no explanation—

it wasn't that.
One night, late,

watching
on a small screen short clips to match

my clipped attention span, I saw an ice shelf
shear off,

glacier's great
plummeting weight,

a scale unfathomable. I'm sure it
made tremendous noise, but I watched on mute,
and that was it.

The closest
I had come.
I admit,
each time

the baby
latched and my

body obliged, beneath the skin-to-skin I felt
the fall of something vast, remote, silent,

and perfectly cold from deeper than inside of me.
It fell into a sea

of its own
substance.
Intimate, yes,
but by intimate, I mean merely made known.

Gwass

is how she says both “grass” and “glass.”
Before she can assemble all three parts
of “delicious,” she shortens it to “wish.”

Revving through gritted teeth to model “R”
for her, I’m a gunned engine, wheels
spinning into snow. Loud past the pressed

tip of tongue, I hold my “L,” sound that,
had we but breath enough, could go on
forever. Snow to mud, mud to grass,

she crouches now to inspect the dandelions’
encroaching constellations. I try to put
my mind where her mouth is, as if each plea

could be its own savored pleasure, as if
I could reconcile the fact that what
shatters is what’s growing as we speak.

Early Evening

From her highchair in Banditos,
a broken chip in each hand, her gaze lifts toward the row

of painted skulls above the door.
I watch her

study the rank-and-file rainbow
of the dead, taking in their shadowed

sockets over lipless grimaces before
finally deciding what they are:

happy babies
wearing sunglasses.

I could try to provide
context or tell her something true of what's inside

of us.
Instead, I look to the low sun streaming through the window and say *yes,*

see, it's still very bright outside.
I promised a past self I would resist the shielded, sanitized,

but now I lose my nerve, buy us
another minute in which the worms are just

resting in the puddles
and the bees are sleeping on the sills.

Passing the junk shop later
on the walk home I let her

point to a perch behind patinaed bars—*birdhouse!*
—and even repeat after her *yes, a birdhouse,*

when all I'd have to say
is *cage*.

Monumental Life Building

The name, a gauntlet thrown down Chase and Charles
Streets, rendering each pedestrian just that—ordinary,
transient, wondering what veined stone sourced
from what dark quarry, what winch and hoist and
labor, might suffice to build a monumental life?
And what so vast that hasn't taken its tithe or more,
tip of a worker's finger or more, capillary-christened?
Up the road, a now-bare plinth shrugs perpetual
disavowal of past purpose where—*look!*—my daughter
(smallest in her class) pointed one afternoon as
a young man hopped atop it to juggle in its statue's
absence. I can still feel her other hand in mine and
somehow, too, the quick palm-thud and twitch aloft
of his brief constellation.

For My Friend Who Is Tired of Children in Poems

I also tire of children in poems and of children
off the page as well. I turn from a line's easy awe
to endless demands, sticky hands at my hem.

My teacher wrote aleph, bet, vet, gimel, dalet, then
dripped honey on top, let the pupils lick the letters.
The line's low buzz metabolizes slowly in the body.

Friend, no one is looking. Bend your head and taste.
Can I call you baby? Can I call you honey only here
on a page white as any side of a cube of refined sugar?

These are just words. Blame me, but it's in my blood
to love this way. I make a study of it. What luxury.
Together, let's be sick of the sweetness of this world.

Rearview Mère

One lump or two? is a Leppard lyric I suspect
no one has heard in full outside a moving vehicle
since this century's turn, but even a window
cracked and the Leppard cranked can still confect me,
spin me a drive-by sugar sculpture CarLotz wife,
sucralost, neck stuck on swivel past the slashed
prices, mouth ajar at a buzzing's searchlight
sweep across these fillings.
                                                What makes 'nother
a mother's obvious: just takes a second
lump. Nursing this mom-fat concoction
scrawled to-go with some off-brand
of my name—Doe-a-dearer, Doe-a-dire,
dorsal fin, fine, *fin*—I admit all I was
willing to sell to sit idling inside a song.

Travelogue

There's a baby's blue car seat up for grabs
on the curb with a hand-lettered sign taped
to the handle: *NO ACCIDENTS.* A part
wants to throw it out into the sea
of traffic just to see context conquer text,
just to say I made some kind of impact.
(Not kind, but some kind of. A part apart.)

The voice of our generation is:
A. reverb in a packed stadium
B. an echo in an empty stadium
C. a playlist on shuffle
D. the form of *I love you*   that your "basic" phrasebook teaches you
      is an *I love you* used only   by lovers.   It's right   under
      Would you like to dance with me?   and right   above
      Get well soon
E. all of the above

or none of?

Time to wake no there is no time to wake should have hours ago dressed
  in the dark
shoes and coats put on then taken off our dark shoes and coats for the
  machine
to better see through us a watch take off the watch that should have
  woken
us hours ago its alarm never set it sets off the alarm we are standing in
our socks cursing the sky as the flight takes flight takes
its place in the pattern without us.

      (all right above all of the all above)

My own mind's mirror
mimes what I want

to see in you
in me.

The news says
    relative success
says
    compensate for past largesse
says
    now less of the "Western-style" excess
says
    offers context on the promise of this moment.

Perhaps it was the echo after all.
Perhaps it was the echo after all.

Time to wake. The higher-ups are trading sleepers.

Still drunk, I see double
agents double going
about their double lives,
double kissing their
double wives goodbye,

goodbye.

Pinch me. A dream's dram: the television
killing time on sci-fi: *I'm okay*
to go. I'm okay to go.

Study questions:
Why did the "thing" take the form
of her father? What is the difference
between agency and department?
Only double? Awfully facile facets, no?

Reverb as verb as in do-over. Dare me.
Was it was more fun for the arbiters before

rewind? Dearly

departed lips

I imagine so

much more.

(more much so imagine I lips departed dearly)

My son would like to meet the pilot would like a pair of plastic wings
pinned to his jacket but the cockpit's locked up tight and the flight
attendant's all business with that beverage cart. *We apologize*
for technical difficulties with the in-flight movie and should
have the problem resolved shortly. On screen, but
silently, a heartthrob sweats his shirt closer to
the contours of his body as he dismantles
a bomb in the bathroom of a moving
train. Which wire? A shot
of hapless passengers.
A shot

of a gun barrel as all else blurs behind it.
In an emergency, light will illuminate the aisle.

TO DO:
stage coup then recoup losses
tell the whole failed truth to strangers
take the bloody coat in to the cleaners
buy milk
buy time
age backward into your arms

Bystanders are standing by.
Did you say red wire?
Cloud's the sky's cover.
There's nothing to see here.

(By force, by farce, they will make sure there's

nothing

to see here.)

Move along, now. Move along.

Mother, may I say and stay preoccupied? Shall we
play a game again to pass the time? How about the one
where "one" means one but "love" means zero?
Or we could write in our breath on the window
XO XO
as valediction becomes beasts of burden
from the vantage point of window's outside looking in.

Whose son would like to meet the autopilot?
Whose son would like to meet the unmanned drones?

My seatmate, a veteran with a purple heart embroidered
over his actual heart, or thereabouts,
tells me: *the cruelest thing God did to us was give us a memory*
tells me: *I don't know why I'm on this side of the grass*

To the left of the still life, an explanation in translation:
Even the dew and waterdroplets have not been forgotten.

I don't believe I don't believe
is not the same as simply faithless

In every version of the story, the blade
finds her neck three times

Is this then what
we call the truth?

The nuns scuttle out to stand above the saints' remains and sing in heterophony. The sky does its decent impression of a ghost. Each starling a grace note, the flock unfolds its unplayable music, glissandi over the bus station, ad libitum. Too young to sit on the piano bench, the child reaches her fists up to pound the keyboard. The dissonance startles her silent. She calls this before and after *song.*

The film of fog, a nictitating membrane,
shields the city's eyes.
You can repel the starlings with recordings
of their own cries of distress.

The sun liquidates its assets, brazen
blazing, taking us all down with it.
CEO, presiding priest, inserts
the usual valediction here, O
most over and misused "Sincerely."

What do we say?

[Silence.]

What do we say when we want something?

So this is the lyric "I" of the lyric storm.
It's awfully quiet in here.

Clearly, there has been a terrible accident.
A foghorn and an empty bench at the edge

of a cliff staring at what we know to be
horizon, now gauzed and bandaged,
immobilized indefinitely. The whole landscape's
in traction. My phone gets no service here,
so if I'm the world's emergency contact,
the world may be waiting a long time.

Inside the accident,
our secret hands shake.
Here, birds are information,
call and recall,
a tainted batch of verbiage.

We have created
the eye that we once thought touched us
with its light, the eye that we once thought
an attic annex one had
to stoop to enter.

Ye shall know them by the mapped
capillaries of the retina,
by the orbits of the fingerprints,
by their digital signatures.

There are two font families by which ye shall know them
　　(*any communication pieces designed with other type fonts*
　　must be approved by Corporate Marketing prior to production.)

I'm no rule breaker.
I'm trying to cry into this
travel-size receptacle.

No film no firearms?

Echoes coo. Why won't the distance think
for itself for a change?
I love that ring too much to wear it.

I confess I fear less that which pursues me
than that which I cannot not hold tight.

I'm sorry to be the breaker but stop looking here on land.
The end of the line in the sand's in the sea.

Ask me to ask me yes or no questions.
Yes, I asked
(the "yes" in "eyes"—the "no" in "now")

I am no blissful bored historian of heaven doing diligence to eternity,
custodian of clean conscience striving to keep blank pages so, so
forever may feast its eyes on the glow of all that need not be said,
storyless storyboard, a row of windows headed past the setting sun
as the airplane banks toward the "See fewer choices" menu option
never to return.

Here's the part where
I rest my case

in your lap. When the agents approach, you have
to insist that you packed it yourself. It's almost true
to tell them that you've always had it with you.

After "After Us"

Others' pity will set out after us
like the moon after some wandering child.
—Nikola Madzirov

Nikola, I owe you a note. So many *one days* in a row
for so many. To answer, finally, I am as fine as anyone
could hope to be within a system's spinning.
I spent a season and another and another watching:
    the neighbor's shows through her window,
    the cases climbing—red bolts of data
        and the rumble that follows,
        dissonant chord of lies and prayers,
    my mouth.
Held tongue chafes, no balm but these same seasons,
embraceless despite the over-armed police.
You begin to end in a last kind wish for me and mine: *I do hope*—
and from afar I borrow a bit of what I need
as any neighbor might, with thanks—

Dear Nikola,
    I do hope too.

Thanks to Johns Hopkins University, Vice Provost for Research Denis Wirtz, and Assistant Vice Provost for Research Julie Messersmith for the JHU Catalyst Award; the William G. Baker, Jr. Memorial Fund, the Baker Artist Portfolios, and the Greater Baltimore Cultural Alliance for the Mary Sawyers Baker Prize; the Amy Clampitt Poet Residency Program, the Amy Clampitt Committee, and the Berkshire Taconic Community Foundation for the Amy Clampitt Residency Fellowship; the Civitella Ranieri Foundation and its Executive Director Emerita Dana Prescott for the Director's Guest Writing Residency; and the American Academy in Rome and its Visiting Artists and Scholars Program. I can't express how much the time, support, and inspiration afforded by these opportunities has meant to me.

With thanks to—and in memory of—Joseph Harrison (1957–2024). Joe, your belief in me meant the world. It was an honor to call you an editor, colleague, and friend. You are still with us in poetry.

Previous titles in the Carnegie Mellon Poetry Series

2012
Now Make an Altar, Amy Beeder
Still Some Cake, James Cummins
Comet Scar, James Harms
Early Creatures, Native Gods, K. A. Hays
That Was Oasis, Michael McFee
Blue Rust, Joseph Millar
Spitshine, Anne Marie Rooney
Civil Twilight, Margot Schilpp

2013
Oregon, Henry Carlile
Selvage, Donna Johnson
At the Autopsy of Vaslav Nijinksy, Bridget Lowe
Silvertone, Dzvinia Orlowsky
Fibonacci Batman: New & Selected Poems (1991–2011), Maureen Seaton
When We Were Cherished, Eve Shelnutt
The Fortunate Era, Arthur Smith
Birds of the Air, David Yezzi

2014
Night Bus to the Afterlife, Peter Cooley
Alexandria, Jasmine Bailey
Dear Gravity, Gregory Djanikian
Pretenders, Jeff Friedman
How I Went Red, Maggie Glover
All That Might Be Done, Samuel Green
Man, Ricardo Pau-Llosa
The Wingless, Cecilia Llompart

2015
The Octopus Game, Nicky Beer
The Voices, Michael Dennis Browne
Domestic Garden, John Hoppenthaler
We Mammals in Hospitable Times, Jynne Dilling Martin
And His Orchestra, Benjamin Paloff

Know Thyself, Joyce Peseroff
cadabra, Dan Rosenberg
The Long Haul, Vern Rutsala
Bartram's Garden, Eleanor Stanford

2016
Something Sinister, Hayan Charara
The Spokes of Venus, Rebecca Morgan Frank
Adult Swim, Heather Hartley
Swastika into Lotus, Richard Katrovas
The Nomenclature of Small Things, Lynn Pedersen
Hundred-Year Wave, Rachel Richardson
Where Are We in This Story, Sarah Rosenblatt
Inside Job, John Skoyles
Suddenly It's Evening: Selected Poems, John Skoyles

2017
Disappeared, Jasmine V. Bailey
Custody of the Eyes, Kimberly Burwick
Dream of the Gone-From City, Barbara Edelman
Sometimes We're All Living in a Foreign Country, Rebecca Morgan Frank
Rowing with Wings, James Harms
Windthrow, K. A. Hays
We Were Once Here, Michael McFee
Kingdom, Joseph Millar
The Histories, Jason Whitmarsh

2018
World Without Finishing, Peter Cooley
May Is an Island, Jonathan Johnson
The End of Spectacle, Virginia Konchan
Big Windows, Lauren Moseley
Bad Harvest, Dzvinia Orlowsky
The Turning, Ricardo Pau-Llosa
Immortal Village, Kathryn Rhett

No Beautiful, Anne Marie Rooney
Last City, Brian Sneeden
Imaginal Marriage, Eleanor Stanford
Black Sea, David Yezzi

2019
The Complaints, W. S. Di Piero
Brightword, Kimberly Burwick
Ordinary Chaos, Kimberly Kruge
Blue Flame, Emily Pettit
Afterswarm, Margot Schilpp

2020
Build Me a Boat: Words for Music 1968–2018, Michael Dennis Browne
Sojourners of the In-Between, Gregory Djanikian
The Marksman, Jeff Friedman
Disturbing the Light, Samuel Green
Any God Will Do, Virginia Konchan
My Second Work, Bridget Lowe
Flourish, Dora Malech
Petition, Joyce Peseroff
Take Nothing, Deborah Pope

2021
The One Certain Thing, Peter Cooley
The Knives We Need, Nava EtShalom
Oh You Robot Saints!, Rebecca Morgan Frank
Dark Harvest: New & Selected Poems, 2001–2020, Joseph Millar
Glorious Veils of Diane, Rainie Oet
Yes and No, John Skoyles

2022
Out Beyond the Land, Kimberly Burwick
All the Hanging Wrenches, Barbara Edelman
Anthropocene Lullaby, K. A. Hays

The Woman with a Cat on Her Shoulder, Richard Katrovas
Bel Canto, Virginia Konchan
There's Something They're Not Telling Us, Kimberly Kruge
A Long Time to Be Gone, Michael McFee
Bassinet, Dan Rosenberg

2023
Night Wing over Metropolitan Area, John Hoppenthaler
Phone Ringing in a Dark House, Rolly Kent
Fleeing Actium, Ricardo Pau-Llosa
Approximate Body, Danielle Pieratti
Wild Liar, Deborah Pope
Joy Ride, Ron Slate
That Other Life, Joyce Sutphen
Sonnets with Two Torches and One Cliff, Robert Thomas

2024
Accounting for the Dark, Peter Cooley
Shine, Joseph Millar
Those Absences Now Closest, Dzvinia Orlowsky
Blue Yodel, Eleanor Stanford
Her Breath on the Window, Karenmaria Subach
Museum of the Soon to Depart, Andy Young

2025
Just About Anything: New and Selected Poems, Jonathan Aaron
The End of the Clockwork Universe, Fleda Brown
Goat-Footed Gods, Kathleen Driskell
Pine, Jonathan Johnson
Requiem, Virginia Konchan
Angel Sharpening Its Beak, Michael McGriff
Trying x Trying, Dora Malech
Markers and Shrines, Margot Schilpp